ONE PLACE AFTER ANOTHER